DOCTORS DID

WHAT?!

The Weird History of Medicine

Richard Platt

TWO CAN ™

MINNETONKA, MINNESOTA

Contents

First published in the USA in 2006 by
Two-Can Publishing
11571 K-Tel Drive
Minnetonka, MN 55343
www.two-canpublishing.com

Editorial Director: Jill Anderson
Cover Design: Brad Norr Design

Library of Congress Cataloging-in-Publication Data
Platt, Richard.
    Doctors did what?! : the weird history of medicine /
Richard Platt.
        p. cm.
    Summary: "Describes medical practices and treatments throughout history, many of which were dangerous, painful, and ineffective"—Provided by publisher.
    Includes bibliographical references and index.
    ISBN 1-58728-580-0 (hardcover : alk. paper) —
    ISBN 1-58728-581-9 (softcover : alk. paper)
    1. Medicine—History—Juvenile literature. 2. Medical innovations—History—Juvenile literature. I. Title.
    R133.5.P53 2006
    610.9--dc22
                                        2006009328

1 2 3 4 5 10 09 08 07 06

Printed in China

**WARNING: The remedies and practices in this book are
for information only and should not be tried at home!**

Introduction

ARE YOU FEELING WELL? Are you sure? Don't worry, the doctor will have you feeling much worse before you can say "blood transfusion." You would never hear this said in a hospital today, but in the past it was dangerously close to the truth. The story of health and healing is stranger and more scary than you might imagine.

Less than 150 years ago, doctors knew how to cure only a few of the diseases that can kill us or make our lives miserable and painful. About 250 years before that, they barely understood anything about how the human body works. And before that, medicine was little more than prayer, luck, magic, and superstition.

It's easy to forget how lucky we are today. Most children born in wealthy countries will grow into healthy adults. When they get sick, medical experts can usually help them get well quickly and without pain. You may complain that the medicine tastes disgusting or the jab in the arm hurts, but once you find out what the sick and injured had to go through in the past, you will never complain again!

Would You Believe...? Would You Believe...?

What, why, when? Why did the ancient Greeks study phlegm? When was the first nose job performed? Why would a doctor drill a hole in your head? How were hares' droppings used as a remedy? When were patients tied down for surgery? If you want to find out the answers, read on!

A Hole
in the Head

HAD YOU LIVED ABOUT 12,000 years ago, the cure for a headache might have been a hole in the head! We don't know very much about how early people treated disease and illness, but we do know that there were some eager amateur **surgeons** around.

Would You Believe...? Would You Believe...?

Lucky charm
Using only stone tools, ancient surgeons scraped then drilled at the skulls of their friends. Amazingly, few of these operations killed the patients. Most people grew new bone over the hole. Some even carried around the cut-away bone as a charm to protect them from bad luck.

The people who performed operations thousands of years ago didn't wear white coats and masks like today's doctors. They wore animal skins and put deer antlers on their heads to make themselves look important and frightening.

▲ **Trepanation tool**
Devices like this were used on battlefields in the 17th and 18th centuries to relieve the symptoms of brain injury.

▲ **True benefits**
In medieval times, trepanning was successfully used to relieve pressure on the brain and remove fragments of bone. This is still done today.

Releasing evil

Ancient doctors relied on religion and magic for their cures. They probably blamed ghosts and evil spirits for disease and pain. Experts believe that early surgeons cut holes in their patients' skulls to release evil spirits from the brain. Cutting a hole in the skull is called **trepanning** or trephining. Archaeologists have found drilled skulls thousands of years old, in places as far apart as France and Peru.

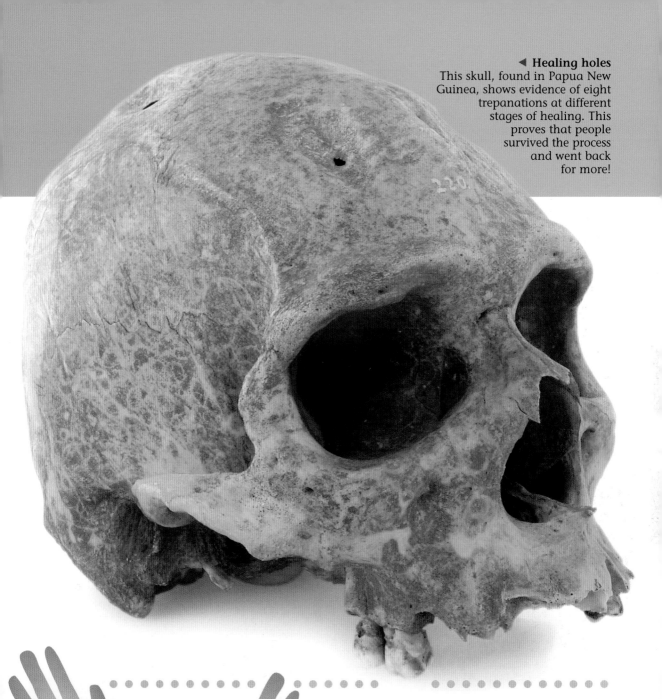

Finger sacrifice
Drawings found in Gargas Cave in southern France may be evidence of another painful ancient cure. Created about 20,000 years ago, the drawings show hands with missing fingers. Some archaeologists believe that local people may have cut off a finger for a magic offering, as a way of curing a bad illness.

Ancient doctors **probably gained their patients' trust with a** crafty **mix of fancy costumes, chanting, and** magic tricks

Road-Dust and Writing

THE STORY OF REAL CURES and healing began some 4,000 years ago in the Middle East. The Mesopotamian people, in the land that is now Iraq, were the first to have real doctors. They still cared for their patients with a mixture of magic and medicine, but they had learned to wash and dress wounds, and operated using sharp copper knives.

To speed healing, Mesopotamian doctors used drugs, some of which had no healing effect at all. Medicines included pills made from lizard dung, but most were made from plants. Doctors found uses for more than 230 kinds of plants, including fig, sesame, laurel, and apple.

The cure for a blow to the cheek was a mouthwash made from the dust of four crossroads

King's code ▶
Much of what we know about Mesopotamian medicine comes from the Code of Hammurabi. This was a list of laws made by the king of Babylon some time before 1750 B.C. It was carved on a tall stone found in the Iranian town of Susa in 1901. Some of the text on the stone says what doctors can and cannot do, and gives the punishments for those who break the law.

Scientists and sorcerers

Mesopotamia had two types of doctors—the ashipu and the asu. The asu prescribed herbal cures, while the ashipu was a spiritual healer and prescribed charms and spells to drive out the demon or god he believed was causing the disease.

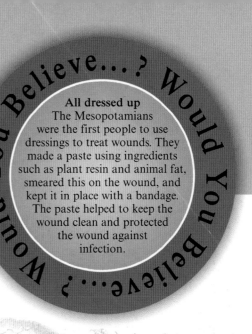

The best Mesopotamian doctors grew rich from their skills. A major operation cost as much as a house. The price of failure was high, too. A surgeon who botched an operation would have his hand cut off.

Treatment of wounds included dressings of river mud

Clay clues ▶
Mesopotamian scribes recorded the cures of both ashipu and asu on clay tablets. This suggests that they valued spells and herbs equally.

◀ Healing hound
The sitting dog was a symbol of healing in Mesopotamia. It took on special meaning 4,300 years ago when rabies, a disease spread by dog bites, struck the land.

Egypt's Sunus

" **H**AIL TO THE high priest Iry, the king's eye doctor, shepherd to the king's bum-hole, doctor to the king's belly!" This was the official title of the most important sunu (doctor) in ancient Egypt 4,300 years ago. His job was to cure aches, pains, wounds, and illnesses everywhere on the royal body.

He was probably not very good at it. Successful cures were usually due more to luck than skill. Sunus did use herbs to heal sickness, but prayers and magic played a bigger part in treatment. This is not surprising. Egyptian doctors had little idea of how the human body worked. They could only guess at the causes of disease, and usually they just blamed evil demons.

First physician ▶
Hesy Re was the first known Egyptian doctor and dentist. There is no evidence that the ancient Egyptians cleaned their teeth, so he must have been a very busy man!

Pelican droppings **and** hippopotamus urine **were among the local animal products used to make pills and ointments**

Beetle power ▶
Most Egyptians could not afford the medical care that sunus offered. Instead, they protected themselves with lucky charms like the scarab beetle, which they believed had healing and protective powers.

The sunus had more success treating injuries and wounds than diseases. The cause of an injury was obvious, and it was clear whether a cure was working or not. The sunus used splints made of bark to set broken bones and help them to heal straight. They also made ointments from grease and honey, which may have worked, too. Modern tests show that honey protects wounds and kills the germs that slow down or stop healing.

Secrets of the mummies

Scientists have learned about the diseases and injuries that afflicted the ancient Egyptians by studying mummies (preserved bodies) found in their tombs and pyramids. Mummies were once used as a cure themselves. Five hundred years ago, European doctors ground them up and sold them as a miracle cure for almost everything.

Cosmetic cure ▶
The funeral mask of the pharaoh Tutankhamen shows how the ancient Egyptians wore lots of eye makeup. This probably helped to protect them from eye diseases. The green and blue colors came from ground-up rock that contained copper. This mineral kills the harmful germs that can infect eyes.

Healing the Greeks

Recovering in ancient greece was a pleasure. You went to relax at a temple called an asklepion (named after the god of medicine). You put gifts for the gods on an altar, put on a blindfold, and slept, dreaming that gods and snakes healed you. You awoke cured, and the gifts were gone. That was the idea, anyway, but one patient peeked: "I spotted the priest taking cheesecakes and figs from the holy table," he wrote.

Medicine god ▶
In Greek mythology, the god Asklepios had exceptional skills in medicine and healing.

Temple treatments did little to cure disease. But by 400 B.C., there was something better. A doctor named Hippocrates was changing how people thought about illness. He was the first to see that diseases came from nature, not from the gods. He noticed that food, climate, and even the work that people did affected their health. Hippocrates believed that if people ate well and rested, their bodies often healed naturally.

There's only one Hippocrates...

Well, actually, there may have been many! Hippocrates gets the credit for ideas that may have come from a whole group of doctors on the Greek island of Cos. The most famous of these ideas is a promise they made to do all they could to heal the sick. Doctors today still take a version of this "hippocratic oath" when they finish medical school.

Medical mistakes

Not all the Greek doctors' ideas were helpful. Some thought that four bodily fluids called **humors** controlled people's health. They believed that sickness arose when there was too much of one humor or too little of another. This was a serious mistake that held back the study of medicine for 2,000 years.

Out of balance ▶
The four humors were **phlegm** (snot), blood, **yellow bile,** and **black bile.** A patient's mood or symptoms helped doctors decide which humor was too strong or weak. They believed, for example, that a high **fever** was a result of excess blood. The treatment for this was **bloodletting—** opening patients' veins to drain their blood.

● ● ● ● ● ● ● ● ● ● ● ● ● ● ● ● ● ●

The Greeks made syringes by tying dried animal bladders to hollow feather quills

Greek pharmacy ▶
Greek doctors knew about some of the drugs we use today, including the pain-killer morphine, which is made from poppy sap. But they also used poisons such as white hellebore, which would have killed more often than it cured.

Would You Believe...? Would You Believe...?

An apple a day
The ancient Greeks had great faith in the healing power of the apple. Apple pulp contains a fiber called pectin, which is good for upset stomachs because it slows down the loss of water. However, the Greeks also knew what they could do with apple seeds. Just a quarter of a cup would kill an adult.

Oriental Wisdom

CLOSING WOUNDS WITH ants' jaws and curing disease with a thousand pinpricks sound like very primitive treatments. But a thousand years ago, doctors who used them in ancient India and China knew much more about sickness and health than doctors in Europe.

Indian medicine was based on a system called Ayurveda, first written down more than 3,000 years ago. Early treatments were the usual mix of superstition and magic. However, by 1000 A.D., Indian doctors had learned some sound lessons about disease and the human body. By practicing with sharp knives on porridge-filled bags, lotus stems, and watermelons, they became experts at surgery. Some even mastered cosmetic surgery and carried out the world's first nose jobs!

The ancient Chinese created herbal cocktails as they tried to make a potion that would give everlasting life

Gory lessons

It was against the rules of the Hindu religion for Indian doctors to **dissect,** or cut up, dead bodies. In order to learn about the human body, they soaked corpses in water for a week. The bodies became so soft that the doctors could brush away the flesh to study the bones and organs inside.

◀ **A stitch in time**
Indian surgeons held up soldier ants to wounds until they gripped the skin around the wound with their pincers and pulled the edges together. The surgeons then snapped off the ants at the waist so that the pincers formed a neat suture, or stitch.

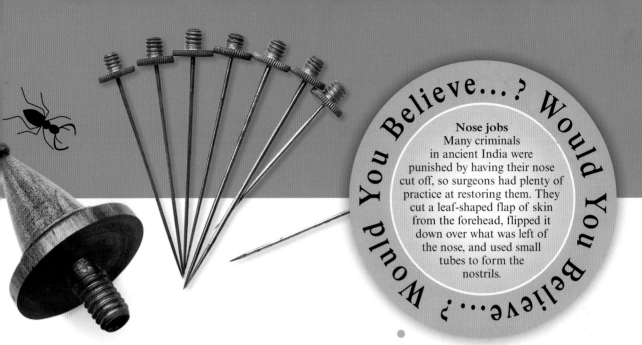

Would You Believe...?

Nose jobs
Many criminals in ancient India were punished by having their nose cut off, so surgeons had plenty of practice at restoring them. They cut a leaf-shaped flap of skin from the forehead, flipped it down over what was left of the nose, and used small tubes to form the nostrils.

Doctors in ancient China aimed to balance life forces called yin and yang. To do this they relied on treatments such as **acupuncture**—piercing of the skin with fine needles—and herbal cures, both of which are still used today.

Pins and plants

Chinese doctors believed that acupuncture helped guide energy around the body, but modern research shows that the needles make the brain release painkilling chemicals into the blood. Chinese herbal remedies are mixtures of plants. Scientists struggle to explain how they cure patients that "ordinary" medicine cannot help.

▲ **Pins and needles**
This set of Chinese acupuncture needles is about 300 years old. The needles are thicker than those used today. Most modern needles are thrown away after use to avoid **infection.**

▲ **Chinese surgeon**
In the second century A.D., Chinese surgeon Hua T'o gained fame for operating on the arm of General Kuan Yun while the man distracted himself with a game of chess. But ultimately, the surgeon's skill led to his death. When a prince called on him for a headache cure, Hua T'o started trepanning. The prince thought Hua T'o was trying to kill him and had the doctor executed.

Flesh of Vipers

Roman water works ▶
The Romans built long bridge-like structures called aqueducts to bring water to the city from up to 57 miles (96 km) away. Each citizen was supplied with 350 gallons (1,325 l) of water a day—more than double that used by people in New York today.

THE PEOPLE OF ANCIENT ROME FELT no need for doctors until 2,300 years ago, when a terrible disease swept through the city. The Romans sent messengers to Greece to seek a cure, and the Greeks gave them a sacred healing snake. As the Roman ship neared home, the snake slithered into the sea. As if by magic, the plague vanished!

The Romans were impressed. From then on, they relied on the Greeks' understanding of the human body. Unfortunately, the Greeks based most of their cures on clever ideas, rather than on their patients' symptoms.

Strange ingredients

A few of the drugs the Romans used did what they were supposed to. For example, ferns killed worms in the digestive system. But for many ailments, Roman **pharmacists** mixed together lots of ingredients, most of which were useless. A popular "cure-all" contained flesh of vipers, pearls, charred stag's-horn, and coral.

Would You Believe...?

Roman cures
Roman folk remedies used things that patients could easily find in the countryside: egg white for cooling sore eyes; pig dung for wounds made by iron; dog's blood for wounds made by poisoned arrows; a mouse cut in two for a snake bite; pellets of goat dung and vinegar for ulcers on the shin.

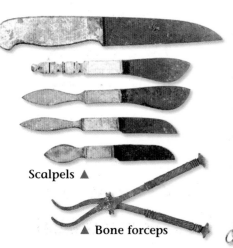

Scalpels ▲

▲ Bone forceps

◀ ▼ ▶ **Soldiers and surgery**
To build an empire that ruled most of Europe, Roman soldiers had to fight hard. Surgeons had plenty of work tending their wounds and became experts at their craft. Some of the instruments used by Roman surgeons would not look out of place in a modern operating room.

◀ **Cupping vessels for bloodletting**

Surgical scissors ▲

Water cures

Medicine didn't improve much while Rome ruled Europe, but health certainly did. And the credit goes not to doctors but to engineers. They designed a system that sent clean river water to drinking fountains and taps in the city of Rome. This put a stop to many of the diseases spread by polluted water.

◀ Gifted Galen
The most famous of all Rome's doctors was Galen. A Greek who came to Rome in 162 A.D., Galen was a brilliant man, writing 600 books on medicine and anatomy—three of them before he was even a teenager! Although his studies taught Roman doctors much about the structure of the human body, he had very fixed ideas. Many were wrong, and his teachings did lasting damage. For example, his belief in the deadly process of bloodletting (see pages 16–17) went on for more than 1,500 years.

Galen learned about blood flow and nerves in the human body by studying and dissecting the bodies of pigs and apes. This led to a few mistakes!

Bleeding and Leeches

Would You Believe...? Would You Believe...?

Blood suckers
Medieval doctors often put blood-sucking creatures called leeches on a patient's body to drain their blood. Leeches are being used in medicine again today, to remove excess blood after skin grafts (transplants) and other surgery. Leech saliva also contains proteins that reduce swelling.

THE BEST CURE FOR disease 1,000 years ago was never to get sick! If you did, prayer was probably the most helpful treatment—there was still little that a doctor could do to help.

To identify illnesses and find their causes, doctors used astrology. To help with this, a handwritten chart hung from every doctor's belt. Some of the charts showed the position of the sun, moon, and planets, which doctors believed could affect a patient's health. Other charts gave a number to each letter of the patient's name. Doctors added them up and subtracted 30 to predict whether a patient would live or die.

The "cure" for almost all diseases was bloodletting

Barber–surgeons ▶
In the 14th century, doctors did not think surgery was a respectable job, so they left it to barbers. One of the practices that barbers performed was bloodletting, illustrated on this wooden barber-surgeon's sign. The barbers advertised their bloodletting services by wrapping a bloody bandage around a white pole. Many barbers today still display a version of this barber's pole, even though they no longer cut open your veins.

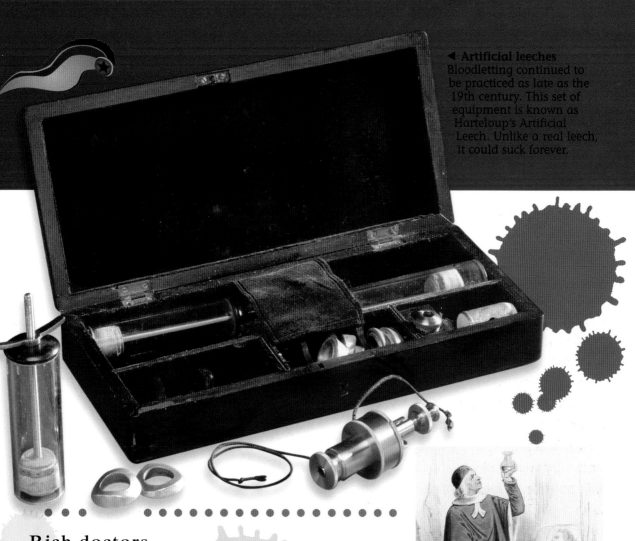

◄ **Artificial leeches**
Bloodletting continued to be practiced as late as the 19th century. This set of equipment is known as Harteloup's Artificial Leech. Unlike a real leech, it could suck forever.

Rich doctors

Doctors grew very rich by practicing medicine. The famous Italian medical school at Salerno told students they would get paid more if they dressed well, rode a good horse, and wore lots of rings. Before treating patients, many doctors made them sign a contract agreeing to the fee. They had found that when patients began to feel better, they often forgot how sick they had been and refused to pay.

The doctor opened a vein and let the patient's blood drain out— a treatment that could not possibly heal a patient, and killed many of them

▲ **Urine and blood**
Medieval doctors thought that studying a patient's urine was useful, and they had guidelines to follow: "Red urine which is muddy shows that the sickness is nearing the end; green urine, coming after red, is a sign of a deadly sickness; urine that is red like blood is a sign of a fever caused by too much blood."

17

Deadly Disease

IT DIDN'T SEEM SERIOUS AT first. Those who caught the disease just felt tired, cold, and prickly to begin with, but a high fever and terrible headaches followed. When painful swelling appeared in the armpit or groin, the person was bound to die. They had the **plague,** also known as "the black death" because it turned the skin dark and blotchy.

Nobody knew how the plague spread. Most blamed air pollution. To relieve "stiff" air, they rang church bells, fired guns, and let birds fly around sickrooms. Some people believed that it was caused by sinful behavior or scanty clothing, and that children caught it as a punishment for being naughty.

▼ Untouchable
Doctors took victims' pulses with a "tickling stick" to avoid having to touch them.

▲ Burning blame
Rumors began to spread that Jewish people were spreading the plague, either by magic or by poisoning wells. Though the stories were obviously untrue, many people believed them and killed hundreds of Jews by burning them alive.

Doctor, doctor!
In 1720, doctors in Marseilles, France, wore a special outfit to protect themselves from the disease. The gown was leather, and the eyes of the mask were glass. Dishonest doctors all over Europe made a fortune selling useless pills that promised a cure.

▲ **Dirty rats!**
Could the plague be so bad again? Probably not. Medical experts think that fleas living on rats spread the disease. Killing the rats or fleas stops a major outbreak, and modern drugs can cure people.

Would You Believe...? Would You Believe...? Would You Believe

Dancing mania
Fear of the plague made people do all sorts of strange things. In 1374 in Aachen, Germany, crowds danced wildly until they dropped exhausted to the ground. This "dancing madness" also broke out in other towns in Germany, and in the Netherlands and Italy.

The plague swept through Europe repeatedly from the 1300s to the 1600s. There was no cure, but some thought smoking tobacco helped. Others whipped themselves, believing the pain would save them. While a few cases of the disease are still reported today, it is curable with modern drugs.

In the worst wave of the plague, in 1349, one-third of Europe's people died

◀ **It's a cover-up**
Some wealthy people carried scented herbs and flowers in a pomander. They swung the container as they walked to release a sweet smell that hid the more unpleasant odors they came across.

▲ **Plague posy**
Doctors put herbs and spices into the beak of their masks. They hoped that by masking bad smells, they would be protected from infection.

19

An Apple a Day

Would You Believe...?

Warts and all
There were many folk cures for warts. For example: touch each one with a different stone, put the stones in a bag, and drop them on the way to church. Your warts will grow on whoever picks them up. Or rub your warts with meat and bury the meat. As it decays, the warts will begin to disappear.

TO CURE A STY (a swelling near the eye), rub it with your mother's wedding ring or let a dog lick it. To stop bedwetting, eat a hare's droppings or the ash of a burned mouse. For mumps, put an ass's halter on the sufferer and lead him around a pigsty three times.

Treatments like these for common diseases and problems are called folk cures or folk remedies. They sound like hocus-pocus, but less than a century ago, many people relied on them. Even today, some folk remedies are still in use, especially for problems that "real" medicine cannot cure, such as baldness and back pain.

▲ **Frog fixes**
The humble frog has been used as a cure for upset stomachs, toothaches, seizures, and hemorrhoids. It is now being researched as a potential cure for HIV.

▲ **Really healing**
Many folk cures included plants that we now know contain healing chemicals. Willow, for instance, was widely used for fever. It contains aspirin, which doctors still prescribe to bring down a temperature. Some more unlikely cures work, too. Cobwebs really do stop wounds from bleeding. And sugar works as a treatment for hiccups, because sugar makes muscles relax.

Hang a sock full of roasted potatoes around your neck to cure a common cold

Many folk cures are nonsense, but it is easy to see why they were so popular for so long. They were cheap or free to use, so people who could not afford a doctor could treat themselves and their families for next to nothing.

Spells and superstition

Not all folk remedies involved swallowing or applying strange concoctions. In many cultures, people took a more spiritual approach to healing. Some people made use of lucky numbers; others believed in using horrible ingredients such as dung to disgust and drive out the evil spirit causing the illness.

Medicine man ▶
European explorers called the doctors of native Asian, African, and North American cultures "medicine men," but these traditional healers (some of whom were women) did more than hand out cures. They were respected for their magical powers and led rituals and ceremonies, often in special masks and robes. This lion mask made a healer of the Ashanti tribe in Africa seem brave and strong.

◀ Crazy cures
Although they were not scientific, some folk remedies seemed to make sense. Others must have been more difficult to believe. For example, how could cramps be cured by wearing a ring made from the hinge of a coffin?

Battlefield Breakthroughs

CUT AND STABBED, BRUISED AND beaten, warriors of the past suffered terrible wounds. For battlefield surgeons, these injuries were a rare chance to learn more about medicine and become better healers. Norwegian king Magnus the Good (1024–1047) was one of the first to look after his wounded troops. He chose the soldiers with the softest hands to treat the wounded.

The wealthy knights of 15th-century Europe took their own surgeons into battle. But centuries passed before doctors were on hand for ordinary troops.

Prepared for war ▶
Doctors in the U.S. Civil War (1861–65) used painkilling drugs and sterilized their medical instruments to get rid of germs.

Would You Believe...?

Paré's potions
Surgeons used to pour boiling oil into gunshot wounds, but it just made them worse. In 1537, Ambroise Paré ran out of oil and tried rosewater, egg, and turpentine. His patients got better—perhaps because they didn't endure the oil treatment! Paré later added puppy fat, worms, and oil of lilies to his mixture.

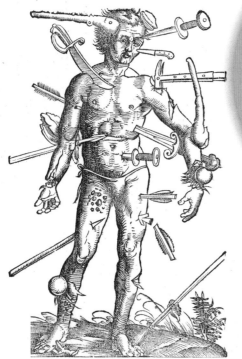

◀ **Wound man**
Hans von Gersdorff (1455–1529) included this gruesome picture in an instruction book he wrote in 1517 to teach surgeons how to treat battle wounds. He also gave the first exact instructions on how to **amputate** (cut off) wounded arms and legs, and printed recipes for soothing ointments.

Wounded soldiers were wide awake while doctors sawed off their limbs

The placebo effect

During World War II (1939–1945), doctor Henry Beecher (1904–1976) ran out of morphine, a powerful painkiller, so he injected wounded soldiers with water. To his surprise, the worthless jab eased their pain. It worked because the soldiers expected to feel better. He called his dummy drug a **placebo**, from a Latin word meaning "I shall please."

▶ **Field hospital**
Doctors in field hospitals during World War II had to work in terrible conditions. There was often little they could do to help the badly injured soldiers brought to them.

Scabs
That Healed

BREATHING IN A FINE powder of ground-up scabs sounds like a horrible way to stop disease, but it works! More than 2,000 years ago, Chinese doctors were able to protect patients from smallpox by making them sniff such a powder.

This deadly disease killed one in every ten children. Those who caught it had a high fever and horrible skin blisters. Scabs formed on the blisters after a week. It was these scabs that the Chinese healers ground up to treat healthy people.

Prepared to fight
We call this way of preventing disease **inoculation** or **vaccination.** Doctors don't do it by blowing scabs up your nose anymore. They are more likely to give you an injection in the arm. This jab infects you with a much weakened form of the disease, called a vaccine. From it the body learns how to fight the real thing.

Queen Elizabeth I of England almost died from smallpox in 1562

Disappearing disease
Western doctors did not learn how to vaccinate people until about 1800, when Edward Jenner (1749–1823) first tried a vaccine for smallpox. Since then, vaccination for smallpox has worked so well that nobody ever catches it anymore.

▼ **Jenner's kit**
These knives were used by Jenner to extract pus from cowpox blisters.

◄ **Jenner's guinea pig**
Eight-year-old James Phipps, Jenner's gardener's son, was the first to receive the new smallpox vaccine.

Smallpox blisters begin in the mouth and spread over the entire body, even affecting the eyes. The scars left behind are known as pockmarks

Doctors today can protect us against many serious diseases by injecting vaccines. Children who are vaccinated can fight the diseases if they come across them later in life.

The needle protects ▶
Vaccination programs are an essential part of aid to developing countries, which may not be able to afford the vaccines without help.

▲ Risky business
Jenner tried his smallpox vaccination after a milkmaid bragged that she couldn't catch smallpox because a cow had given her cowpox, a much less serious disease. Jenner rubbed pus from the girl's blisters into a cut in the skin of a young boy. Weeks later, he tried to infect the boy with smallpox. To his relief, the boy did not get sick.

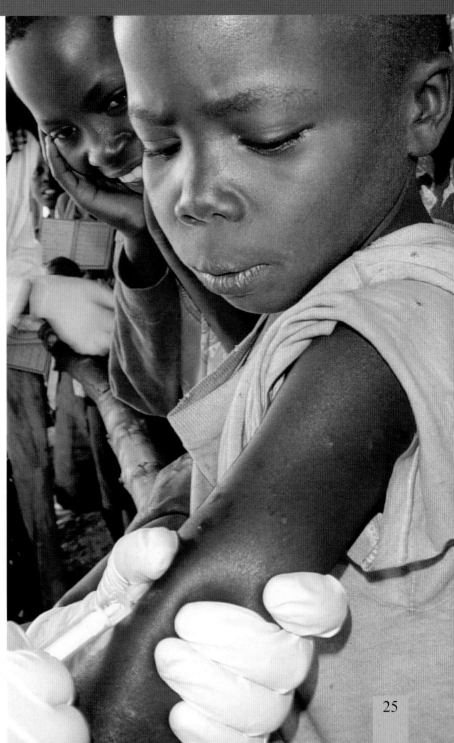

25

Quack, Quack

AT FESTIVALS AND FAIRS IN THE 18th century, there was a show no one wanted to miss. Squeezed in between the fire-eater and the acrobats, a quack doctor was part entertainer, part doctor—and part crook. Quacks got their nickname because they "quacked" (bragged loudly) about their skills. They tricked people into buying "cures" that were usually useless.

One famous quack was Joanna Stephens. She sold the secret of her pills to the British government for 1,600 British pounds ($1.3 million in today's money). They were made from herbs, soap, eggshells, and snail shells, and did not cure anything.

Would You Believe...? Would You Believe...?

Temple of Health

Medical school dropout James Graham was one of the most notorious "doctors" of the 18th century. He opened a clinic in London called the Temple of Health, where patients could take electric baths, be buried in warm earth, sleep in the celestial bed, or be nursed by the goddesses of health.

MORRISONS PILL for EXPORTATION

▼ Sally Mapp
"Crazy" Sally Mapp was enormously strong and very ugly. She pulled dislocated bones back into position.

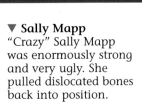

Join the club
Not all quacks were dishonest. A few, such as Crazy Sally Mapp, had real healing skills but were not considered respectable or rich enough to join the doctors' "clubs" that controlled medicine.

URICURE

en las PRINCIPALES DROGUERIAS Y FARMACIAS

REUMATISMO . ARTRITIS GOTA & ARENILLAS

▲ Time reversal
Uricure pills were sold as a miracle cure for the ailments of old age, including arthritis, gout, and rheumatism.

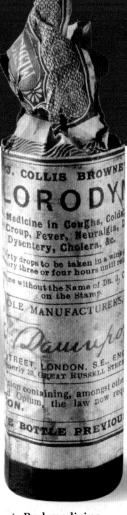

Gustavus Katterfelto was a quack and a magician. He sold a flu cure with help from two "talking" black cats and his daughter (whom he claimed to lift to the ceiling with a magnet). To announce his arrival in a town, two servants walked ahead of his carriage, blowing trumpets and handing out leaflets.

▲ Bad medicine
In the late 1800s, Dr. Collis Browne's popular chlorodyne drops were billed as a cure for everything from toothaches to **cholera**. They dulled the pain, but they also made patients addicted to the opium in the drops.

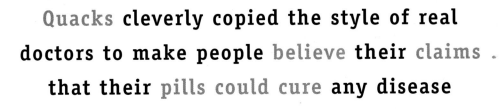

Quacks cleverly copied the style of real doctors to make people believe their claims that their pills could cure any disease

Germ Warfare

I F ODORS CAUSED DISEASE AND mold appeared from nowhere, we would have a hard time staying healthy or keeping food fresh. But just 200 years ago, there were no better ways to explain sickness and rotting. Most people thought that "miasma" (bad smells) made us ill and that rot and maggots just appeared by "spontaneous generation."

The scientist who did the most to prove these ideas wrong was French chemist Louis Pasteur (1822–1895). He showed that molds did not grow on their own. Something in the air was causing the decay. That "something" was what we now call **germs** or microbes (tiny animals and plants).

▲ ▼ Animal doctor
Pasteur experimented with animal diseases. He infected cows and chickens with weakened versions of serious diseases. Pasteur found that the animals fought off the minor infections, and this seemed to protect them against the full-blown form of the disease.

Pasteur studied yeast— a fungus that makes beer brew and bread rise

The human touch

When he began to look at human sickness, Pasteur read about Edward Jenner and vaccination (pages 24–25). He started searching for a way to weaken diseases so that he could use them as vaccines. By 1882 he had succeeded, making vaccines to protect people against three deadly diseases: cholera, anthrax, and rabies.

▲ Flasks and filters
Pasteur showed that dust in the air contains germs. He boiled some broth in a special U-shaped flask, then placed cotton in the neck to keep air from getting in. No mold grew. But when he removed the cotton plug, the broth soon turned moldy.

Deadly dog
Rabies is a disease spread to humans by animal bites. Pasteur had been working on a vaccine for years when a nine-year-old boy who had been bitten by a rabid dog was brought to him. Pasteur knew the boy would die without help, so he injected him with a weak form of the disease. It saved his life.

National hero ▶
Pasteur died a hero. He was given a state funeral at Notre Dame Cathedral in Paris, France.

Pasteur died in 1895, but you see his name every day—on milk jugs and cartons. Pasteur showed that heating milk killed any germs it contained. This process, called **pasteurization** in his honor, is still used to keep milk fresh.

A LOUIS PASTEUR

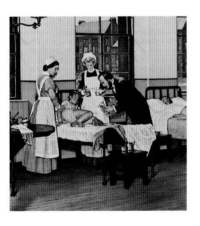

◀ Killing germs
When English surgeon Joseph Lister (1827–1912) heard of Pasteur's work with germs, he saw that it could save lives in the hospital where he worked. Nearly half of his patients died after surgery when their wounds turned **septic**, or rotted. Lister began cleaning wounds and spraying operating rooms with carbolic acid, a chemical that kills germs. Soon only one in every seven of his patients was dying.

Before Lister, operating rooms were full of germs—surgeons wore ordinary clothing and no masks

Speedy Surgery

IF THE IDEA OF SURGERY makes you feel weak and ill, imagine what it would be like to have an operation when you were wide awake, with nothing to dull the pain of the surgeon's knife. This is what surgery was like for most of human history. It was a terrifying ordeal. Most people agreed to it only if the alternative was death or a life of constant pain.

After the pain of surgery came the risk of infection. Without clean conditions and modern drugs, the wounds left by surgery could turn septic, killing the patient.

Would You Believe...?

Born under the knife
Childbirth in ancient times was a dangerous business. When a baby was too large to pass through its mother's hips, a surgeon could cut open the mother's belly in a "cesarean" procedure. This saved the baby but often killed the mother. Cesarean surgery does not carry the same risk now.

▼ **Painful stones**
Doctors feared cutting into the body, but the removal of bladder stones was an exception. The constant pain caused by the crystals was so bad that patients risked surgery and its brief pain to relieve it. This instrument was used in about 1780 to reach into the bladder and grab the stones.

Painful work

Almost as frightening as the knife itself was the preparation for surgery. Patients were tied down to the operating table to keep them still. Then four strong men gripped their arms and legs. Because the pain was so terrible, surgeons worked as quickly as they could. Some of them could saw off a patient's leg in less than a minute.

Medical school ▶
Roger of Salerno was a medieval surgeon who specialized in spinal, brain, and nerve surgery. These images come from his book of surgical techniques, written in the 12th century.

▲ Leg lopping

This 19th-century amputation set contains useful tools for cutting off an arm or a leg. Amputation was the most common operation, and wars gave surgeons lots of practice at it. Without amputation, many soldiers and sailors would have died from a bad wound to an arm or leg.

Most people saw a priest before they faced the surgeon's knife

Killing Pain

TO DULL THE TERRIFYING pain of surgery, patients used herbal drugs or drank alcohol until they were senseless. Nothing really took away the pain until 1846, when American dentist William Morton gave a remarkable demonstration at a hospital in Boston, Massachusetts.

Morton joined a surgeon for an operation. Before surgery began, he gave the patient a chemical called **ether** to breathe. Within seconds, the man was fast asleep, and the surgeon set to work. The audience expected the man to scream in agony, but he didn't stir.

The patient lay silent and still as the knife cut deep into his flesh

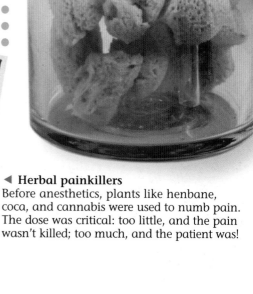

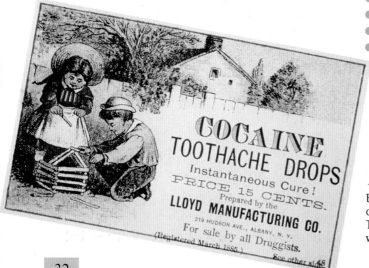

◄ **Herbal painkillers**
Before anesthetics, plants like henbane, coca, and cannabis were used to numb pain. The dose was critical: too little, and the pain wasn't killed; too much, and the patient was!

Medical breakthrough

Morton had demonstrated something surgeons had only dreamed of. Ether was an **anesthetic**: a substance that made patients fall into a deep sleep in which they did not feel pain. His discovery changed medicine forever.

Would You Believe...?

Laughing gas
Another anesthetic, a gas called nitrous oxide, came into use about the same time as ether. It was nicknamed "laughing gas" because it made people feel unusually happy. One person who enjoyed nitrous oxide said that it "made you feel like the sound of a harp."

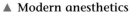

▲ **Modern anesthetics**
Ether was safe and fairly effective, but it has since been replaced with anesthetics that work faster and put patients into an even deeper sleep. They are injected into a patient's bloodstream or are given through a mask.

In William Morton's demonstration in Boston, the patient stayed asleep until Morton took away the ether. Then the astonished audience rushed to question him. "Did you really feel nothing?" they demanded. "Only a sensation like that of scraping with a blunt instrument," the man replied.

33

Vitamins and Veggies

Would You Believe...?

Scurvy cures
Scurvy became common only when European sailors began to make really long ocean journeys in the 16th century. However, a few people suffered from it even in ancient Rome and Egypt. The Egyptian cure was rather less tasty than lime juice—they used onions. The Romans preferred cabbage.

D O YOU WONDER WHAT would happen if you never ate any vegetables? Sailors from the 16th century knew all about it. They would run out of vegetables soon after leaving port. After four weeks, they felt weak, then their gums bled, their teeth loosened, and their skin turned purple. Before they died, all their old scars opened up.

Ships' officers believed the causes of the disease, known as **scurvy,** included kissing girls and breathing the stale air of the cramped decks where men slept. Remedies included burying sick sailors up to their necks in cold earth and washing the decks in vinegar. Nothing worked.

▲ **Getting your vitamins**
Citrus fruits like oranges, lemons, and limes are high in vitamin C. One orange contains about 70 mg of vitamin C— the perfect amount for keeping you scurvy-free.

Super juice

As early as 1653, a ship's surgeon suggested that a lack of fresh vegetables caused scurvy, but a century passed before anyone paid attention. Then, British admiral James Lind (1716–1794) showed that feeding sailors lime juice prevented the disease. By 1800, a disease that sometimes killed nine out of ten sailors had virtually disappeared.

▼ **Victims of war**
During World War I, abandoned Russian children were forced to survive on a diet of "famine bread" made of clay, grass, and leaves. The children were reduced to skin and bones, and many suffered from scurvy.

Scurvy grass ▲
This coastal plant was eaten by sailors returning from long voyages to relieve the symptoms of scurvy. Its leaves have a peppery taste and are loaded with vitamin C.

We now know that to stay healthy, our food must contain small amounts of chemicals called **vitamins.** It is the vitamin C in fruit and vegetables that prevents scurvy. Since Lind's time, scientists have found many more vitamins and named each with a letter. Learning your food alphabet could save you from a nasty death!

AQUA COCHLEAR

Bad Water,
Good Water

TURN ON THE TAP, AND FRESH water gushes out. Clean water is vital for life, but over a billion of the world's people still can't get any. Nor could people 150 years ago. London had the worst water of any city. **Sewage** flowed into the Thames River, which was also the source of drinking water!

In the 1800s, half of all children in London died before the age of five. Most of them died of diseases caused by drinking contaminated water. Regular outbreaks of **cholera,** one of the diseases spread by sewage, killed up to 14,000 Londoners each year.

The Thames River was black and stinky. Anyone falling in it died not of drowning but of poisoning

◀ **Flush it and forget it**
London's sewage problems were partly caused by the flush toilet. Until people started installing this invention in the late 18th century, houses had cesspits, or sewage tanks. Night-soil men took away the solid material from these pits to sell to farmers as fertilizer. The toilet changed this, allowing people to flush sewage straight into the river.

In the summer of 1858, the smell from the Thames was unbearable—it was called "The Great Stink." The city's lawmakers ordered engineers to build sewers to carry London's filth safely away, and a separate network of pipes was built to bring in clean water for drinking from far upstream. After that, there were no more cholera outbreaks in London.

Good water

Water is no "magic cure," as people once believed, but drinking more clean water can help relieve ailments from kidney stones to constipation.

◀ Ancient water cures

Images of water spirits are carved near many mineral springs. This one is from Bath, England. Belief in the healing power of water continues to this day.

● ● ● ● ● ● ● ● ● ● ● ● ● ● ●

Would You Believe...? Would You Believe...? Would You Believe...?

Marine medicine

A trip to the seaside doesn't seem like a reliable cure for anything, but in the 1800s, people believed visits to the beach would improve their health. An English doctor started the craze for "sea cures" in 1752, and resorts called marine hospitals soon sprung up along the coast.

▼ Deadly pumps

Sewage seeped from the Thames into wells, killing people who drank the water from them. When Dr. John Snow (1813–1858) discovered that a well in Soho was spreading cholera, he had the pump handle removed so that no one could draw water from it.

▼ Cholera kit

Doctors tried to treat cholera with medicines, but it was the discovery that it was linked to dirty drinking water that saved the most lives.

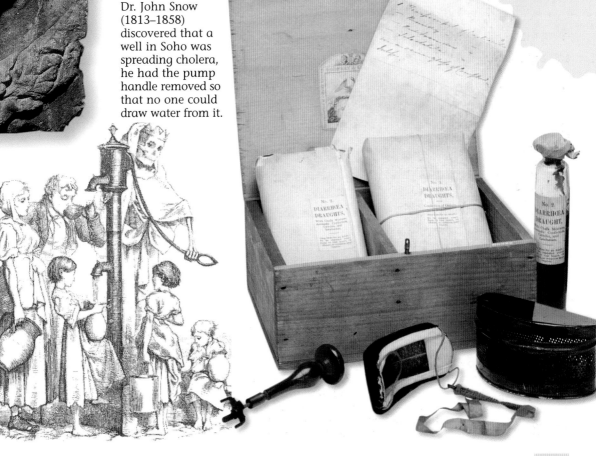

Magical Mold

I N A CLUTTERED LABORATORY IN England, an Australian scientist struggled to make mold grow. His equipment included a bathtub, milk churns, bedpans, lemonade bottles, a bookshelf, and a mailbox. In 1940, as war raged across Europe, Howard Florey and his assistant Ernst Chain announced a great discovery: the world's first **antibiotic** drug, penicillin.

▲ **Fleming's lab**
Florey made penicillin after reading about the work of a bacteriologist named Alexander Fleming. Twelve years earlier, Fleming had returned from vacation to find a strange mold growing in one of his laboratory dishes. The mold had killed **bacteria** growing nearby. Fleming realized that his discovery was important, but he had stopped work on it when he failed to turn the mold into a useful drug.

In 1945, Fleming, Florey, and Chain shared medicine's greatest award—a Nobel Prize— for the discovery of penicillin

Florey and Chain tried out their drug in February 1941 on a dying policeman. With each dose he got a bit better, but they did not have enough to cure him. To make more, they collected his urine and extracted the penicillin that had passed through his body. The policeman died, but Florey and Chain made more penicillin, tried again, and cured eight people.

▼ **Florey's drug factory**
In his junk-shop factory, Howard Florey first grew mold and extracted the penicillin it produced. He concentrated the drug by freeze-drying it, then purifying it until it was safe to inject in humans.

Life savers

Florey and Chain knew their drug could save lives, but they had a big problem. They made the drug from liquid that oozed from penicillin mold, and it took a bathtub of the liquid to make one drop of the drug. They went to the United States for help. There, scientists figured out how to grow the mold more quickly—on slices of melon! By the time the war ended in 1945, there was enough penicillin to treat all the wounded soldiers from Britain, the U.S., and their allies. Antibiotics have since saved millions more lives.

Mad or Bad?

Would You Believe...? Would You Believe...? Would You Believe...?

The talking cure
Austrian doctor Sigmund Freud began treating mentally ill patients in 1881. He encouraged them to talk to him about the experiences that had made them unwell. Then he could understand and help them. His "talking cure" was the first psychotherapy. Some of his methods are still used today.

MENTALLY ILL patients may look normal and seem healthy, but they are as sick as someone with a rash, a fever, or a gaping wound. Today, drugs and therapy can help patients get well, but for much of history the only treatment was exorcism —a religious ceremony designed to get rid of the "demons" people thought caused their problems.

Most mentally ill patients got no treatment at all. They were labeled "idiots" or "lunatics" and locked up in madhouses such as London's Bethlehem Hospital. These facilities attracted many visitors. For an entrance fee, anyone could go and stare at the terrified inmates.

▼ The madhouse
Today, any scene of crazy confusion is described as "bedlam." The word comes from the shortened name of the most famous madhouse, Bethlehem Hospital in London. It started taking in mentally ill people in 1377. Patients were chained up, often naked, and punished for violence by being ducked in cold water or whipped.

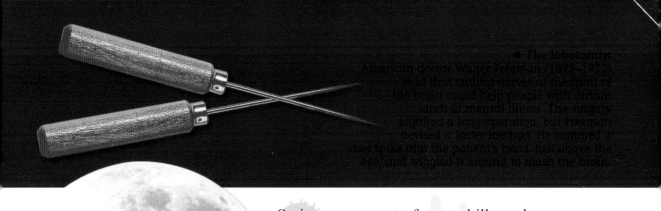

◄ The lobotomist
American doctor Walter Freeman (1895–1972)
read that cutting nerves at the front of
the brain could help people with certain
kinds of mental illness. The surgery
required a long operation, but Freeman
devised a faster method. He rammed a
steel spike into the patient's head, just above the
eye, and wiggled it around to mash the brain.

Serious treatment of mental illness began
in the 19th century, but this did not entirely
stop the cruelty. As late as 1950, doctors
were "operating" on the brains of the
mentally ill with iron spikes and hammers.
This crude surgery, called **lobotomy,**
caused terrible brain damage.

Some children were lobotomized for being disobedient or for getting a bad report card

▲ **Lunatics**
People once believed that a full
moon made mental illness worse.
They called the illness lunacy and
its sufferers lunatics, from the Latin
name for the moon, *lunaris.*

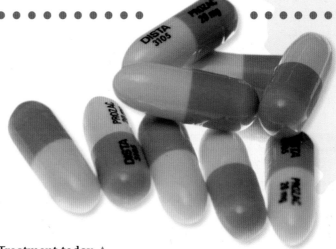

Treatment today ▲
Fortunately, treatment of mental illness today is kinder
and works better than in the past. Mind-altering drugs,
first used in the 1950s, can cure patients with some forms
of mental illness. Drugs can make seriously ill patients
feel better and help them to lead normal lives.

Shocking Discoveries

▼ **Defibrillator**
Used scientifically, electricity saves many lives. This modern defibrillator machine shocks heart-attack victims to get their hearts beating again.

WHEN SCIENTISTS first began studying electricity, they believed that this invisible force would unlock many of the mysteries of medicine. After all, in one of the first electrical discoveries, Italian Luigi Galvani (1737–1798) made a frog's leg twitch by passing electricity through it.

In later experiments, scientists amazed audiences by creating huge sparks like lightning. Surely anything with such power must affect the body!

Body electric

People in the 19th century were impressed by the magnets, sparks, and health claims, and rushed to buy "electrotherapy" machines. At best, these devices gave patients a harmless, tingling electric shock. But some, such as electric belts and electric corsets, did nothing. The "therapy" was no more than a trick for making money from people who believed that they were ill.

Medical electric machine ▶
Like hundreds of similar "medical electrical" machines, this one delivered an impressive but useless shock to anyone who gripped the handles.

▲ **Electric corset**
Lined with wires, the electric corset was said to cure kidney, liver, and bladder troubles, and backaches. Curiously, women felt no sensation—perhaps because it was doing nothing.

We now understand more about electricity in our bodies. We know that electrical currents flowing in our **nerves** allow us to feel pain and move our muscles, and that our thoughts are really flashes of electrical power.

The sparks and crackles of electricity made it the perfect quack cure

Back to the
Age of Ignorance

MODERN MEDICINE can do amazing things. It can protect us from diseases that would once have killed us in days. Surgeons can save our lives by giving us a new heart or kidneys. Smart drugs can even deliver cures that are personally tailored to each of us.

But doctors still cannot cure everything, and growing numbers of desperate patients are turning to the past for a cure. Even people who may be cured with modern drugs are trying alternative remedies—sometimes with great success.

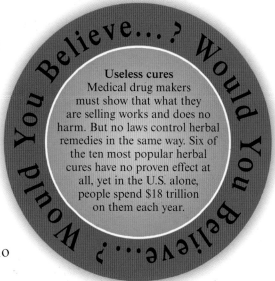

Would You Believe...? Would You Believe...?

Useless cures
Medical drug makers must show that what they are selling works and does no harm. But no laws control herbal remedies in the same way. Six of the ten most popular herbal cures have no proven effect at all, yet in the U.S. alone, people spend $18 trillion on them each year.

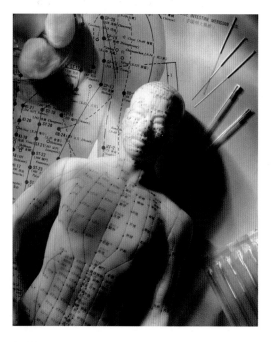

◀ **Acupuncture**
Brain scans of treated patients show that the ancient Chinese needle-prick treatment really does relieve pain for some people.

Looking forward
Some alternative remedies work, even if scientists cannot explain why, but others do not. They come from a time when guesswork, astrology, religion, and superstition were the only cures for the sick. By turning away from modern medical knowledge, we throw away a thousand years of progress.

Some alternative remedies have brought back the tricks of the 18th-century quacks

Find Out More

You can find out lots more about the history of medicine from these books and websites.

Books

Barnard, Bryn. *Outbreak! Plagues That Changed History.* New York: Crown, 2005.

Fradin, Dennis Brindell. *We Have Conquered Pain: The Discovery of Anesthesia.* New York: M. K. McElderry, 1996.

Giblin, James Cross. *When Plague Strikes: The Black Death, Smallpox, AIDS.* New York: Harper Trophy, 1997.

Kent, Deborah. *Snake Pits, Talking Cures, and Magic Bullets.* Brookfield, Conn.: Twenty-First Century, 2003.

Marrin, Albert. *Dr. Jenner and the Speckled Monster: The Search for the Smallpox Vaccine.* New York: Dutton, 2002.

McClafferty, Carla Killough. *Head Bone's Connected to the Neck Bone: The Weird, Wacky, and Wonderful X-ray.* New York: Farrar, Straus, Giroux: 2001.

McCoy, Bob. *Quack! Tales of Medical Fraud from the Museum of Questionable Medical Devices.* Santa Monica, Calif.: Santa Monica Press, 2000.

Murphy, Jim. *An American Plague: The True and Terrifying Story of the Yellow Fever Epidemic of 1793.* New York: Clarion, 2003.

Websites

Learning from the past
www.schoolscience.co.uk/content/4/biology/abpi/history/
An interactive timeline of medicine, from 8000 B.C. to the present day.

Doctor over time
www.pbs.org/wgbh/aso/tryit/doctor/#
This website from the Public Broadcasting Service shows how doctors from the past treated different ailments.

Dream Anatomy
www.nlm.nih.gov/exhibition/dreamanatomy
An introduction to how people have drawn and painted the organs, muscles, and bones of the human body, from the National Library of Medicine.

Smallpox
www.nlm.nih.gov/exhibition/smallpox
This site tells the story of the killer disease and how it was wiped out forever.

Kidswork
www.knowitall.org/kidswork/hospital/
Find out about medicine from the past and learn what goes on in today's hospitals.

Glossary

acupuncture a Chinese therapy that involves inserting fine needles into the patient's skin in order to relieve pain

amputate to surgically remove a wounded limb, such as an arm or a leg

anesthetic a chemical that keeps a patient from feeling pain

antibiotic a drug (such as penicillin) that kills bacteria and cures infections

bacteria the smallest of living creatures, some of which cause disease in humans, animals, and plants

black bile one of the four humors, or bodily fluids, first described by Hippocrates in ancient Greece, associated with depression

bloodletting a process in which a vein is opened to let blood flow out, in the mistaken belief that it willl cure illness

cholera (CAW-ler-ah) a deadly disease causing vomiting and diarrhea. It is spread by polluted water.

dissect (DIE-sect) to cut up a dead body in order to study its structure

electrotherapy a medical treatment that uses electricity

ether (EE-thur) a chemical liquid, the vapor of which sends those who breathe it into a deep sleep. It is used as an anesthetic.

fever a higher-than-normal body temperature caused by illness

germ any tiny plant or animal that can cause illness

humors four fluids that the people long believed kept the body healthy if they were all present in the right quantities. They include phlegm, blood, yellow bile, and black bile.

infection the invasion of the body by germs, often causing disease

inoculation a procedure in which a person is exposed to a dead or weakened form of a disease, as a way of protecting him or her from getting a full case of the disease in the future

lobotomy (low-BAH-tuh-mee) a medical procedure in which part of the brain is deliberately damaged or removed

nerve one of many threads in the body that carry the electrical signals to and from the brain and spinal cord and control muscle movement

pasteurization the heating of a liquid to kill harmful germs

pharmacist someone trained in the use or the making of drugs

phlegm (FLEM) a sticky fluid produced by the nose and lungs. As one of the four humors first described by Hippocrates, phlegm was associated with cold and weakness.

placebo (pluh-SEE-bo) a harmless substance given to a patient to make them believe they are receiving a real drug

plague (PLAYG) the name for diseases that spread quickly, killing many people

scurvy a disease caused by a lack of vitamin C

septic rotting

sewage household waste, including urine and feces

surgeon a doctor trained in cutting open the body to cure illness inside it

trepanning a procedure in which a doctor drills a hole in the skull

vaccination a procedure in which a dead or weakened form of a disease is injected into a person, as a way of protecting him or her from getting a full case of the disease in the future

vitamin one of a number of chemicals essential to health, which are found in small amounts in food

yellow bile one of the four humors, or bodily fluids, first described by Hippocrates in ancient Greece, associated with anger and irritability

Index

Photo credits

The publisher would like to thank the following for their kind permission to reproduce their photographs:

Position key: c=center; b=bottom; l=left; r=right; t=top

Cover: Photodisc/Punchstock

1: NHPA/James Carmichael Jr; 4c: Musée d'Histoire de la Médecine, Paris, Archives Charmet/Bridgeman Art Library; 4tr: Bettmann/Corbis; 5t: Wellcome Library, London; 6cl: Bookwork/Darren Sawyer; 6r: Art Media/Heritage-Images; 7l: The British Museum/Heritage-Images; 8bc: TopFoto.co.uk Werner Forman Archive; 8–9b: Bookwork/Darren Sawyer; 9r: Sandro Vannini/Corbis; 10cl: Mary Evans Picture Library; 10–11c: The British Museum/Heritage-Images; 12b: Michael & Patricia Fogden/Minden Pictures/FLPA; 13l: © Copyright the Trustees of The British Museum; 13r: Wellcome Library, London; 14bl, 14bc, 14br: Courtesy of Historical Collections & Services, Claude Moore Health Sciences Library, University of Virginia; 15b: Mary Evans Picture Library; 15t: Vanni Archive/Corbis; 16: Science Museum/Science & Society Picture Library; 17cr: Science Museum Pictorial/Science & Society Picture Library; 17t: Science Museum/Science & Society Picture Library; 18bl: Christel Gerstenberg/Corbis; 18r: Bettmann/Corbis; 19bl: Bookwork/Darren Sawyer; 19c: Private Collection/Bridgeman Art Library; 20r: NHPA/James Carmichael Jr;

21r: TopFoto.co.uk Fortean 1933/ERG; 22bl: Wellcome Library, London; 22–23t: Tria Giovan/Corbis; 23br: University of Virginia Visual History Collection, Special Collections, University of Virginia Library; 24bl: Courtesy Pfizer Inc; 24bc, 24br: Science Museum/Science & Society Picture Library; 24–25c: Science Museum/Science & Society Picture Library; 25r: Jean Pierre Aim Harerimana/Reuters/Corbis; 26: Wellcome Library, London; 27tc: Wellcome Library, London; 27tr: Science Museum/Science & Society Picture Library; 28b: Science Museum/Science & Society Picture Library; 29bl: Courtesy Pfizer Inc; 29tr: Oxford Science Archive/Heritage-Images; 30–31b: Ann Ronan Picture Library/Heritage-Images; 30–31c: Science Museum/Science & Society Picture Library; 31t: Science Museum/Science & Society Picture Library; 32bl: Corbis; 32–33c: Science Museum/Science & Society Picture Library; 33tr: Pete Saloutos/Corbis; 34b: Bettmann/Corbis; 34tr, 35tl: Bookwork/Darren Sawyer; 35r: Wellcome Library, London; 35tc: TH Foto-Werbung/Science Photo Library; 36bl: Bettmann/Corbis; 36–37tc: Ann Ronan Picture Library/Heritage-Images; 37br: Science Museum/Science & Society Picture Library; 38cl: Wellcome Photo Library; 39tl: The British Library/Heritage-Images; 39br: Wellcome Library, London; 40–41b: Wellcome Library, London; 41br: Najlah Feanny/Corbis; 41cl: NASA; 41t: Wellcome Library, London; 42t: Sotiris Zafeiris; 42–43c: Science Museum/Science & Society Picture Library; 43tr: Mary Evans Picture Library; 44bl: William Whitehurst/Corbis